MW01253002

FOOD

Poetry

Selected by
Robert Hull

Illustrated by
Annabel Spenceley

Wayland

Thematic Poetry

Animal Poetry
Christmas Poetry
Day and Night Poetry
Food Poetry
Green Poetry
Houses and Homes Poetry
Science Poetry
Sea Poetry

Series editor: Catherine Ellis
Editor: Susannah Foreman
Designer: Derek Lee

First published in 1992 by
Wayland (Publishers) Ltd
61 Western Road, Hove
East Sussex BN3 1JD, England

© Copyright 1992 Wayland
(Publishers) Ltd

**British Library Cataloguing in
Publication Data**
Food Poetry. — (Thematic Poetry Series)
I. Hull, Robert II. Spenceley,
   Annabel
III. Series
821.008
ISBN 0-7502-0617-9

Picture Acknowledgements
The publishers would like to thank the following for allowing their illustrations to be reproduced in this book: The Bridgeman Art Library 12; Greg Evans Photo Library 36; the Hutchison Library 5, 9, 25, 34, 39, 42; Oxford Scientific Films *back cover*, 22, 26; Papilio Photographic 18; Edward Parker *front cover*, Reflections (Jennie Woodcock) 21; Tony Stone Worldwide 7, 16, 31; Wayland Picture Library 28, 32.

Acknowledgements
For permission to reprint copyright material the publishers gratefully acknowledge the following: Bodley Head for 'Sugarcane' from *I din do Nuttin* by John Agard; Cambridge University Press for 'Hunger' from *Yarouba Poetry* ed. Ulli Beier; Jonathan Cape for 'Little Bits of Soft Boiled Egg' from *A Child's Book of Manners* by Fay Maschler, and 'Point of View' from *Where the Sidewalk Ends* by Shel Silverstein; Rebecca Gaskell for 'Sharing Figs'; HarperCollins Publishers for 'Hot Cake' by Shu Hsi, trans. by Arthur Waley, from *Chinese Poems*; The National Exhibition of Children's Art for 'Baby Breakfast' by Julia Marsden from *The Cadbury Second Book of Children's Poetry*; Terry Lee for 'Me Aunty Connie', from *Down to Earth and On Its Feet*; Zara Page for 'Blessing in Disguise'; 'Blue Peter' from *Live Album* by Mick Gowar, copyright © Mick Gowar, 1990, first published by Viking Kestrel, 1990, published by Penguin Books 1991; 'Sink Song' (p242) by J. A. Lindon from *Yet More Comic and Curious Verse* (1959) selected by J. M. Cohen, copyright © J. M. Cohen 1959, reproduced by permission of Penguin Books Ltd.; 'Water' (p122-3) by Sa'di Yusuf from *Modern Poetry of the Arab World* (1986) trans. and ed. by Abdullah al-Udhari, translation copyright © Abdullad al-Udhari, 1986, reproduced by permission of Penguin Books Ltd.; Irene Rawnsley for 'The Hungry Burglar'; Rita Ray for 'I didn't want to come to your party anyway'; University of Chicago Press for 'Pleasures' from *Greek Lyrics* (1962) no 747, trans. R. Lattimore; Anvill Press Poetry Ltd for 'Pig' from *Vasko Popa: Complete Poems* (1993), trans. Anne Pennington, revised and expanded by Francis R. Jones; Heinemann Ltd for Jack Prelutsky's 'My Younger Brother's Appetite' from *Something has been Here*; Virago Press Ltd for 'The Health Food Diner' from *And Still I Rise* by Maya Angelou.
Typeset by Dorchester Typesetting Group Ltd, England
Printed in Italy by G. Canale & C.S.p.A., Turin

Contents

Introduction

One poem in this book says, 'There is no god like one's stomach; we must sacrifice to it every day.' You might not have thought of your stomach as a god to sacrifice to, but the idea seems right, doesn't it? Poetry often looks at things in unusual ways. Shel Silverstein thinks about Thanksgiving and Christmas dinners 'from the dinner's point of view'; Joan Downar even imagines a fly feeding on blackberries.

Because poets look hard at life around them, even ordinary things can seem different. That's why poetry, like life, is full of surprises. You might think about cake in a new way after you've read Terry Lee's story of 'The Senior Cream Dolloper'. But poets are ordinary people too. Like you, when they think about food they think mainly about eating it. They write about eating sugarcane or figs – and their pleasure makes you feel you're eating while you read.

Food means hunger too, if you don't have any. Sa'di Yusuf, an Iraqi poet, talks of the children whose only 'drink' is 'the smoke of missiles'.

At the other extreme, food means, for some, sheer greed. Writing in the sixteenth century, Edmund Spenser draws an unforgettable picture of a disgusting glutton: 'His belly was up-blowne with luxury, And eke with fatnesse swollen were his eyne.'

Food can also be funny, of course. Or, rather, what people do with it can. Food can get in the strangest places . . . babies can do interesting things with their dinners.

So, if you stick your head inside this book, like a horse with a nose-bag, you can partake of an amusing old sausage (called a 'bird') or a hot cake or some little bits of soft-boiled egg. Because poetry is a kind of food, too. You might not need to sacrifice to the god of poetry every day, but your mind can soon go hungry as well as your body. In a balanced diet, you need poems with your potatoes.

On Making Tea

The water bubbles
Should become happy;
Not angry.

The tea leaves
Should become excited;
But not violently so.

The pouring of the water
On the leaves
Should be a conception;
Not a confusion.

The union of tea and water
Should be allowed to dream;
But not to sleep.

Now follow some moments of rest.

The tea is then gently poured
Into simple, clean containers,
And served before smiling
And understanding friends.

R. L. WILSON

Hunger

Hunger makes a person lie down –
He has water in his knees.
Hunger makes a person lie down
And count the rafters in his roof.
When the Muslim is not hungry he says:
We are forbidden to eat monkey.
When he is hungry he eats a baboon.
Hunger will drive the Muslim woman from the harem
Out into the street.
Hunger will persuade the priest
To steal from his own shrine.
'I have eaten yesterday'
Does not concern hunger.
There is no god like one's stomach:
We must sacrifice to it every day.

ANON.
(Translated from the Yoruba by Ulli Beier)

Little Bits of Soft-Boiled Egg

Little bits of soft-boiled egg
Spread along the table leg
Annoy a parent even more
Than toast and jam dropped on the floor.
(When you're bashing on the ketchup
Keep in mind where it may fetch up.)
Try to keep the food you eat
Off your clothes and off your seat,
On your plate and fork and knife.
This holds true throughout your life.

FAY MASCHLER

Gluttony

And by his side rode loathsome Gluttony,
   Deformed creature, on a filthie swine,
   His belly was up-blowne with luxury,
   And eke with fatness swollen were his eyne,
   And like a Crane his necke was long and fyne,
   With which he swallowed up excessive feast,
   For want whereof poor people oft did pyne;
   And all the way, most like a brutish beast,
He spued up his gorge, that all did him deteast.

In greene vine leaves he was right fitly clad;
   For other clothes he could not weare for heat,
   And on his head an yvie girland had,
   From under which fast trickled downe the sweat;
   Still as he rode, hc somewhat still did eat,
   And in his hand did bear a bouzing can,
   Of which he supt so oft, that on his seat
   His dronken corse he scarce upholden can,
In shape and life more like a monster, than a man.

Unfit was he for any worldly thing,
   And eke unable once to stirre or go
   Not meet to be of counsell to a king,
   Whose mind in meat and drinke was drowned so,
   That from his friend he scarcely knew his foe:
   Full of diseases was his carcas blue,
   And a dry dropsie through his flesh did flow:
   Which by misdiet daily greater grew:
Such one was Gluttony, the second of that crew.

EDMUND SPENSER

luxury *rich living*
eke *also*
gorge *contents of stomach*
yvie *ivy*
meet *fit, or suitable*

13

Sugarcane

When I take
a piece of sugarcane
and put it to me mouth
I does suck and suck
till all the juice come out.

I don't care
if is sun or rain
I does suck and suck
till all the juice come out.

But when I doing homewuk
and same time playing bout
Granny does tell me,
'How you can work properly
and play at the same time?
Your brain can't settle.
I always telling you
you can't suck cane and whistle,
you can't suck cane and whistle!'

JOHN AGARD

Point of View

Thanksgiving Dinner's sad and thankless
Christmas Dinner's dark and blue
When you stop and try to see it
From the turkey's point of view.

Sunday dinner isn't sunny
Easter feasts are just bad luck
When you see it from the viewpoint
Of a chicken or a duck.

Oh how I once loved tuna salad
Pork and lobsters, lamb chops too
Till I stopped and looked at dinner
From the dinner's point of view.

SHEL SILVERSTEIN

Pleasures

Loveliest of what I leave behind is the sunlight,
And loveliest after that the shining stars, and the moon's face,
But also cucumbers that are ripe, and pears, and apples.

PRAXILLA
(Translated from the Greek by
Richmond Lattimore)

Water

The lark drinks
The star drinks
The sea drinks
The bird
And the house-plant drink
But the *Sabra* children
Drink the smoke of missiles.

SA'DI YUSUF
(Translated by Abdullah
al-Udhari)

From *The Bramble Hedge*

It is two o'clock. The pin-head spider
is sure his life is long, long
as his six legs. The fly,
feeding on blackberries is convinced
he is meeting God, eye to eye.

JOAN DOWNAR

My Younger Brother's Appetite

My younger brother's appetite
is finicky, and very slight,
he's almost guaranteed to hate
whatever's placed upon his plate.
'I will not eat these greens!' he groans,
'This chicken has too many bones,
the cantaloupe is far too sweet,
there's too much gravy on the meat.'

He whines, 'The salad tastes like soap,
the macaroni's more like rope,
I cannot stand these soggy peas,
and I won't touch this awful cheese!'
My younger brother doesn't eat
enough to fill a parakeet.
However did he get to be
the size and shape of two of me?

JACK PRELUTSKY

Pig

Only when she felt
The savage knife at her throat
Did the red veil
Explain the game
And she was sorry
She had torn herself
From the mud's embrace
And had hurried that evening
From the field so joyfully
Hurried to the yellow gate.

VASKO POPA
(Translated by Anne Pennington)

The Hungry Burglar

The house stunk of sheep
when we came home;
a cold draught
blew through the kitchen.

'Burglars,' Dad said,
'or a tramp,
by the smell in here.
Let's see what he's taken.'

Like thieves
we searched our house;
camera, rings, money,
Jamie's little piggy bank;
all still there.

Only a loaf
fresh baked that afternoon
was cut in two;
one crumbly half still stood
on the kitchen table.

'He must have been hungry
to take just bread,' said Mum.
'If we'd been home
I'd have given him cheese as well,
and a mug of tea.'

Sitting by the fire later
we made toast,
two buttered pieces each,
but I couldn't eat
for thoughts of the hungry man
keeping warm with sheep.

IRENE RAWNSLEY

Blue Peter

'I'll just run through the recipe again:

Any nuts without the shells
(Unsalted peanuts only, please remember),
Millet (stripped) and sunflower seeds –
Or any packet wild-bird seed is fine.

Mix thoroughly and weigh.

Add half the weight of melted fat.
Lastly, stir it all together
And put it in the fridge to set.'

A wild-bird cake.
To keep the birds alive in this,
The coldest winter anyone remembers,
Is easy. A child can do it.

Ten minutes later on the News:
Another day of pensioners found
Dead from cold
In London, Glasgow, Manchester . . .

A million children – maybe more –
Still watching.

MICK GOWAR

27

FOOD POETRY

28

I didn't want to come to your party anyway

May your jelly never wobble
May your custard turn to lumps
May your toffee go all gooey
And your mousse come out in bumps

May your pancakes hit the ceiling
May your cocoa crack the cup
May your lollies turn to water
And your sponge cake soak it up

May the icing on your birthday cake
Set hard as superglue
And they'll tell me 'Wish we hadn't
Been invited – just like you!'

RITA RAY

On a Sunday

On a Sunday, when the place was closed,
I saw a plump mouse among the cakes in the window:
dear ladies,
who crowd this expensive tea-room,
you must not think that you alone are blessed of God.

CHARLES REZNIKOFF

The Health-Food Diner

No sprouted wheat and soya shoots
And Brussels in a cake,
Carrot straw and spinach raw,
(Today, I need a steak).

Not thick brown rice and rice pilau
Or mushrooms creamed on toast,
Turnips mashed and parsnips hashed,
(I'm dreaming of a roast).

Health-food folks around the world
Are thinned by anxious zeal,
They look for help in seafood kelp
(I count on breaded veal).

No Smoking signs, raw mustard greens,
Zucchini by the ton,
Uncooked kale and bodies frail
Are sure to make me run.

Loins of pork and chicken thighs
And standing rib, so prime,
Pork chops brown and fresh ground round
(I crave them all the time).

Irish stews and boiled corned beef
And hot dogs by the scores,
Or any place that saves a space
For smoking carnivores.

MAYA ANGELOU

Hot Cake

Winter has come; fierce is the cold;
In the sharp morning air new-risen we meet.
Rheum freezes in the nose;
Frost hangs about the chin.
For hollow bellies, chattering teeth and shivering knees
What better than hot cake?
Soft as the down of spring,
Whiter than autumn floss!
Dense and swift the steam
Rises, swells and spreads.
Fragrance flies through the air,
Is scattered far and wide,
Steals down along the winds and wets
The covetous mouth of passers-by.
Servants and grooms
Throw sidelong glances, munch the empty air.
They lick their lips who serve;
While lines of envious lackeys by the wall
Stand dryly swallowing.

SHU HSI
(Translated by Arthur Waley)

Sausages

The sausage is a cunning bird
With feathers long and wavy
It swims about in the frying pan
And lays its eggs in gravy.

ANON.

Blessing in Disguise

Give us this day
Our daily bread
Before it is
Irradiated

ZARA PAGE

Hodge's Grace

Heavenly Father bless us,
And keep us all alive,
There's ten of us for dinner
And not enough for five.

ANON.

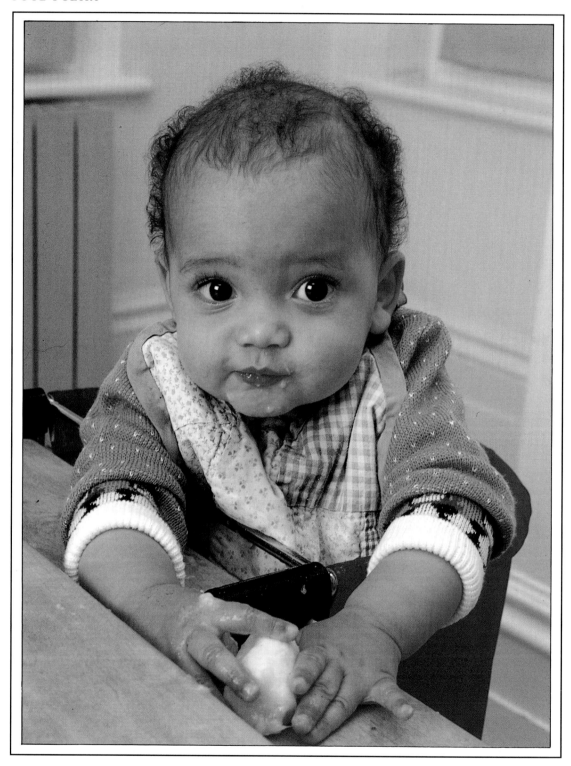

Baby Breakfast

Squidge
My food in my fist
Throw
It at the wall
Rub
It in my hair
Soak
It in my milk
Squeeze
The dirt out
Stuff
It in my mouth
Splurt
It across the room
Dig
It out of my bib
Catapult
It at Mummy
Aim
It at Daddy
Mmmm
Finished.

JULIA MARSDEN
(Aged 15)

Me Aunty Connie

They made cakes at Carson's.
Enormously sticky ones.
With dollops of cream on top,
Jam tarts and doughnuts
Fancy eclairs,
All made at Carson's,
Me Aunty worked at Carson's
On the cream button.
She put the dollop on the cake
As it passed along the conveyor belt.
She'd been there fifteen years
Then she was promoted
To Senior Cream Dolloper.
It carried responsibility,
And extra buttons.
She had to ensure
No cakes were eaten.
It was instant dismissal at Carson's
To eat a cake.
Laughing and talking
Was also forbidden.
If she'd stayed
Another fifteen years,
She'd have been promoted again
To the packing machine
What puts the cakes in boxes,
To take them to the shops.

But she didn't stay.
She was offered a higher paid job.
And on her last day,
She dolloped the wrong cakes.
And the Chelsea buns
Went through with cream on them,
While the gateaus went without.
And the foreman blew his whistle
And stopped production.
The emergency light went on
And the manager came down.
Everyone was laughing and talking.
When he asked her why she did it,
She said because she wanted to.
Course she got dismissal instantly.
But she didn't care.
On the way out,
She picked up a cake
And ate it in front of him.
Everyone at Carson's
Knows me Aunty Connie.

TERRY LEE

41

Sharing Figs

I reach
from an uneasy ladder
in the fig-leaves' dark,
their rasping
touch on my face,
disturbing several
red admirals
that flutter
their way out,

pull down bulky
softening fruit –
purple, deep red,
some split white
down their sides –
nudge
two down
accidentally
splat open.

I leave hard
green fruit
for later,
abandon
the raddled wasp –
and starling-eaten.

I climb down,
count out
the first fruit
on the garden table,
hold one – soft,
sacky, hours ripe –
to my mouth,
drinking it
head back
empty
from underneath,

and drinking count
twelve red admirals
on the tree-summit,
three under it,
wings spread
over figs fallen,
drinking
with me.

REBECCA GASKELL

43

Sink Song

Scouring out the porridge pot,
    Round and round and round!

Out with all the scraith and scoopery,
Lift the eely ooly droopery,
Chase the glubbery slubbery gloopery
    Round and round and round!

Out with all the doleful dithery,
Ladle out the slimy slithery,
Hunt and catch the hithery thithery,
    Round and round and round!

Out with all the obbly gubbly,
On the stove it burns so bubbly,
Use the spoon and use it doubly,
    Round and round and round!

J. A. LINDON

Biographies

John Agard was born in Guyana in 1949. He became a well-known poet, and came to England in 1977. One of his books, *Say It Again, Granny*, is full of poems that he has written using Caribbean proverbs.

Maya Angelou was born in 1928 in St Louis, USA. She has been a waitress, singer, actress, dancer, writer and mother. As well as writing for newspapers in Egypt and Ghana, she has published novels and short stories, several books of poetry, and an autobiography in five volumes that has become famous.

Joan Downar is an ex-librarian and teacher who lives near Nottingham. This poem comes from her second book, *The Old Noise of Truth*, published by Peterloo Poets in 1989.

Rebecca Gaskell was born in 1935 in the north of England, and writes poems for children and adults.

Mick Gowar lives in Cambridge. 'Blue Peter' comes from his new book *Live Album*.

Julia Marsden was 15 when she wrote the poem here. It was published in Cadbury's *Second Book of Children's Poetry* in 1984.

Zara Page, who comes originally from Lancashire, now lives in Hampshire, where she teaches and lectures in art and design. She paints landscapes in watercolour, and writes poems and stories.

Vasko Popa was born in 1922 in Grebenac, Yugoslavia. His poems have won prizes in several countries and been translated into many languages.

Praxilla was a Greek poet who lived in the fifth century BC. Only a few of her poems have survived.

Jack Prelutsky has written over 30 books of verse and is the USA's best-selling poet. He spends much time reading his poems to children in schools and libraries throughout the USA.

Irene Rawnsley lives in Settle, N. Yorkshire. She has written two books of poems for children, *Ask a Silly Question*, and *Dog's Dinner*, both published by Methuen and Mammoth.

Rita Ray lives in Cheshire, with her husband and cats. She writes poems, stories and books for teachers, and also works as a writer-in-school.

Charles Reznikoff was born in Brooklyn, New York, in 1894. He was at one time a lawyer, then worked in Hollywood, and finally became a freelance writer. He died in 1976, just before his *Complete Poems* was published.

Sa'di Yusuf was born in Basra, Iraq, in 1934. After training to be a teacher he left Iraq for Beirut, and in 1982 moved to Cyprus, where he now lives.

Shu Hsi was a Chinese poet who lived in the third century AD.

Shel Silverstein was born in Chicago in 1932. He is one of the most popular children's poets in the USA, and is also a composer, a cartoonist and a folk singer.

Edmund Spenser was a famous English poet who lived in the sixteenth century. He wrote one of the longest poems in English, called 'The Faerie Queene'.

The Yoruba are a people of many millions who live in Western Nigeria and other parts of West Africa. They are famous for their poetry and music.

Index of first lines